Compulsive Eating: The Struggle to Feed the Hunger Inside

Compulsive Eating:
The Struggle to Feed the Hunger Inside

Christie Ward

THE ROSEN PUBLISHING GROUP, INC.
NEW YORK

The Teen Health
Library of
Eating Disorder
Prevention

Published in 1998 by The Rosen Publishing Group, Inc.
29 East 21st Street, New York, NY 10010

Library of Congress Cataloging-in-Publication Data

Ward, Christie.
Compulsive eating: the struggle to feed the hunger inside / Christie Ward
        p.   cm. — (Teen health library of eating disorder prevention)
Includes index.
Summary: Discusses the social and psychological causes of compulsive eating and provides guidance for those struggling with this problem.
ISBN 0-8239-2763-6
1. Eating disorders—Social aspects—Juvenile literature. 2. Eating disorders—Psychological aspects—Juvenile literature. [1. Eating disorders.] I. Title. II. Series.
RC552.E18W37 1998
616.85'26—dc21   97-46782
                                                                          CIP
                                                                           AC

Manufactured in the United States of America

Contents

Introduction

Food. You can't live without it. But to be healthy and happy, you need to know how to live with it.

Unfortunately, food has become a serious problem for millions of people in the United States. Many people have an unhealthy relationship with food. About 60 to 80 million Americans suffer from obesity. This means they have an excess of body fat, which can result in health problems. Another 8 percent of Americans suffer from serious eating disorders. Because the social pressure on young females to be slim and model-like is particularly strong, more than 90 percent of those with eating disorders are teenage girls and young women.

The two best-known eating disorders are anorexia nervosa and bulimia nervosa. Anorexia is a condition in which a person fears being fat and refuses to eat—losing excessive amounts of weight. Bulimia is when a person binges, or eats large amounts of food, and then purges, or gets rid of the food by vomiting or using laxatives and other drugs.

Compulsive exercise is also considered a serious eating disorder-related problem. This is when a person constantly exercises to get rid of calories. This behavior is also known as exercise bulimia, because the person is using exercise to purge food from her system. However, there is a third and more common food-related problem called compulsive eating (also known as binge eating disorder).

Like those suffering from bulimia, compulsive eaters consume much more food than their bodies can use. But unlike bulimia sufferers, compulsive eaters do not purge the food they eat. While some compulsive eaters stay thin by exercising or fasting for long periods of time, most are overweight. That means they must live with the prejudice of a society that believes everyone should (and can) be thin. They must also live with the emotional problems that result from this belief.

Much in the way that alcoholics are addicted to alcohol, compulsive eaters are addicted to, or hooked on, food. Their lives are controlled by thoughts of what, when, and how much they will eat. As a result, many compulsive eaters are also addicted to dieting. They believe diets can help them control their obsession with food. Typically, they become yo-yo dieters, constantly losing and regaining weight in an unhealthy way.

Compulsive eaters are not alone in thinking of themselves as good when they are eating low-fat foods and losing weight and as bad when they are eating fattening foods and gaining weight. Many people feel guilty about what they eat, but those who eat compulsively take these feelings to an extreme. They feel so guilty about their lack of self-control about food that they often eat alone or they hide their food and eat it secretly. They eat whether or not they are hungry. They often consume large amounts of sweets and high-calorie foods and do not stop until they feel uncomfortably full. Compulsive eaters usually feel ashamed of their bodies and judge themselves and the way they eat in a harsh and unkind manner.

Most teenage girls and many teenage boys have probably experienced some of the problems described above. It is nearly impossible to live in a culture obsessed with fitness and thinness without having a negative body image at least some of the time. However, teens who suffer from compulsive eating are never free of these bad feelings.

No matter how smart, talented, or decent they are, compulsive eaters feel that their problems with food and weight make them unworthy of the fun, friendship, and happiness that other teens share. They struggle to fill an empty space in their lives with food, but the hunger inside can never be satisfied unless they start to change the way they think about themselves, the feelings that prompt them to overeat, and the amounts and types of food they eat.

If you think you may be a compulsive eater or in danger of becoming one, or if you know someone who is struggling with overeating, this book will help you understand the problem better and find help in dealing with it. It is important to know that this is not a diet book. Nor does it offer quick and easy cures. However, it does discuss some of the cultural, social, and personal factors that can trigger compulsive eating, and it provides guidance for teens who want to find long-term solutions to this painful problem.

The Myth of the Ideal Body

Ask a group of people to describe the ideal body and you'll probably hear a variety of answers: the name of a famous model or celebrity, or maybe a set of measurements, a description of the size and shape of certain body parts. One answer you will surely never hear, not even from models and movie stars, is, "The ideal body is my body."

Nearly everyone who believes that there is an ideal body describes it as thinner, stronger, healthier, and better than his or her own. The ideal body is always something that we lack, something we can never achieve—not with diets, pills, or even plastic surgery. In other words, the ideal body is always impossible because we can never allow ourselves to believe that our own bodies are ever good enough.

Cultural Ideas About Fat and Thin

Do you sometimes wake up in the morning, look in the mirror, and say, "I feel fat today." But how can you *feel* fat? Fat is not a feeling, like happiness, sadness, excitement, or fear. When you say, "I feel fat," you are not really talking about the size of your body. Instead, you are telling yourself, "I'm not good enough."

Maybe you are nervous about a test at school or afraid nobody will ask you to the school dance. Maybe you feel like an outsider with your classmates or you are having problems with your parents. These situations can be difficult to deal with, and you may find it easier to blame your body for all of your bad feelings. Maybe you believe that all your problems would disappear if you were thinner.

It is easy to see why people become dissatisfied with or take things out on their bodies when they experience problems. We live in a culture that teaches us that we should never be happy with the size and shape of our bodies. Everywhere we look—in the movies, on television, in magazines and newspapers, on billboards and other advertisements—we get the message that fat is bad and unhealthy while thin is beautiful and healthy.

The fashion sections of magazines for girls and women show ultra-thin models wearing the latest styles, leading most teens to feel that their own bodies are not good enough. Then the health and fitness sections of the same magazines seem to offer help by promising a thinner, smaller body after just a few weeks on some fad diet. But the slimness featured in magazines is impossible for most of us to achieve. People come in a variety of shapes and sizes, and each type of body has its own beauty. It's easy to forget that the slim figures featured in magazines are just one particular body shape.

Although slimness is in fashion today, that hasn't always been the case. In past centuries, a full, fleshy

The media portray a very unrealistic ideal body type. Most people don't realize how much these messages affect their self-image.

It's difficult to reject the false notion that what we look like is a true reflection of who we are.

body was considered desirable because it signified wealth, beauty, and fertility. For example, paintings by the great seventeenth-century masters of Western art, Rembrandt and Rubens, feature big, beautiful women.

Plump was popular for female figures until a few decades ago, and in the 1950s and early 1960s, a full-figured Marilyn Monroe was America's most celebrated sex symbol. It is only in the last twenty or thirty years that our nation's obsession with slimness has become so intense and widespread.

The Changing Roles of Men and Women

Although both males and females suffer from a poor

13

self-image, the problem is particularly difficult for girls because the female body naturally has a higher percentage of body fat than the male body. As they grow older, girls develop a protective layer of fat on their breasts, tummies, and hips in preparation for their child bearing years, while boys' bodies grow firmer and more muscular.

These differences are healthy and natural. But the changing roles of men and women in our society have helped create an unhealthy myth of the ideal body. Women have advanced in traditionally male areas of life, such as business and sports. But some critics argue that people have come to expect that women's bodies should be more like men's—hard, strong, and muscular—in order for women to perform as well as men in these areas. Such demands are unhealthy and often impossible.

Peer Pressure

The myth of the ideal body can be particularly troubling for teens because the teenage years are full of difficult physical, emotional, and social changes. Puberty can be especially difficult for girls because their bodies naturally put on more weight to prepare for menstruation. Many teens feel that they will not be popular if they have the wrong body shape. But most are unaware that genetics play a big part in determining their body shapes.

Teens with bodies that don't fit naturally into the current ideal often fear that they will never be sexually attractive to anyone. Well-meaning friends and family sometimes make these insecurities worse by suggesting dangerous solutions, such as fad diets and diet pills. The real solution is for teens to learn to love and accept themselves—no matter what their body size or shape—and find healthier ways to deal with food and feelings.

Feelings About Food

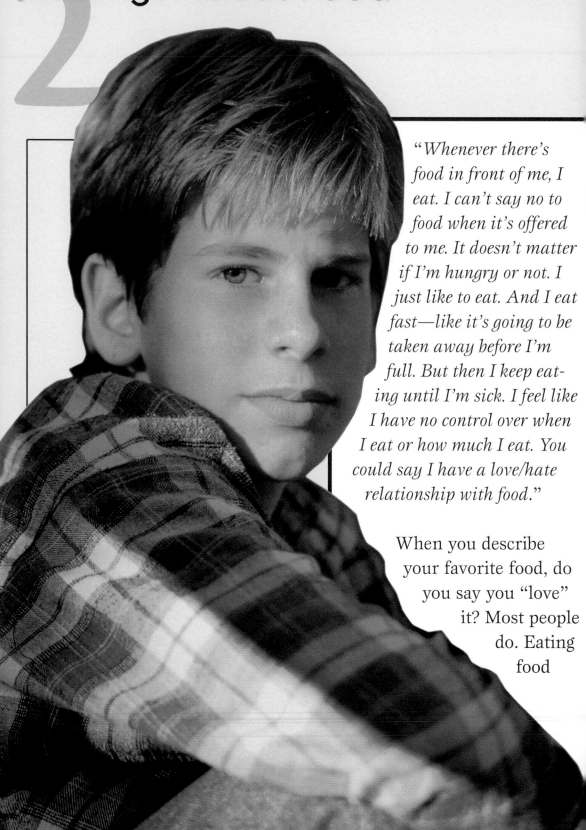

"Whenever there's food in front of me, I eat. I can't say no to food when it's offered to me. It doesn't matter if I'm hungry or not. I just like to eat. And I eat fast—like it's going to be taken away before I'm full. But then I keep eating until I'm sick. I feel like I have no control over when I eat or how much I eat. You could say I have a love/hate relationship with food."

When you describe your favorite food, do you say you "love" it? Most people do. Eating food can be a very sensual experience. Your sense of taste is involved, of course, but so are your other four senses. Your sense of sight is pleased when you look at a beautiful piece of fruit, for instance, and your sense of smell is awakened by the scent of bacon frying. Opening a can of cola and listening to the fizz, or chomping on a bag of crisp potato chips, involves your sense of hearing. Licking a smooth, cold ice cream cone excites your sense of touch.

There is nothing wrong with enjoying the way food arouses all of your senses. In fact, it is a good idea to be mindful of the food you eat. If you allow yourself to enjoy each bite of food, it is easier to feel satisfied and to know when you have had enough.

Unfortunately, people who suffer from compulsive eating often don't take time to enjoy their food. They eat because they want to feel full, much in the way that alcoholics drink because they want to feel drunk. But while a person can quit drinking, people who are addicted to food cannot quit eating to solve their problems. As a result, feelings about food become complicated for the compulsive eater.

Food as Necessity

Food is necessary for human life. We need a balanced diet to feed our bodies and maintain nutritional health. Our ancestors had to grow or kill their own food to survive, and their diets were simple.

Sometimes there wasn't enough food, and people got sick and died. Today, most of us can go to a grocery store or restaurant and buy whatever we want to eat. At fast-food restaurants, we can get food without even leaving the car. Pizza parlors and Chinese restaurants deliver to our homes. Food is readily available, plentiful, and convenient, and we can pick what we want from foods grown and manufactured all over the world.

One of the results of having all these choices is that eating has become an important part of our social life, and many people have developed a love/hate relationship with food. Although we are a culture obsessed with health and fitness, millions of us are struggling with what and how much we eat. Our feelings about food have become a national problem.

Comfort Foods

Often, the foods that we love most are comfort foods—familiar foods that seem to make us feel better when we eat them. They may be foods that our mothers or grandmothers made for us when we were small, or foods that we ate during holidays or on special occasions. They remind us of times when we felt happy, warm, safe, and loved.

While there is nothing wrong with eating foods that you associate with happy memories, you must be careful not to confuse food with emotion. Food is

Most of us learn to attach feelings to food when we are young. Parents may use food to reward or punish their children.

the fuel that you use to keep your body running. It does not have the power to make you feel good or bad—only you have that power. Sometimes you can get confused, though, and start to think that food is a cure-all, that it can make everything okay when you have a problem. When this happens, comfort foods become a dangerous drug, and you start to lose control over your own eating.

"Good" Foods and "Bad" Foods

When we are very small children, "good" foods are foods we like and "bad" foods are foods we don't like. As we get older, food takes on different meanings. We learn these meanings from our parents. As we start to worry about our weight, we learn that "good" foods are low-fat, low-calorie foods like vegetables, fruits, and grains, and "bad" foods are high-fat/high-calorie foods like sweets, fast foods, and fried snacks or meals.

We say that we are being good when we eat low-fat/low-calorie foods and bad when we eat high-fat/high-calorie foods. For example, a person might say, "I was good today. I only ate a salad." Another might say, "No, I can't have any dinner because I was bad this afternoon. I ate a whole bag of potato chips." Unfortunately, many of the foods that we thought of as good when we were small children are the same foods that we're supposed to think of as bad when we get older.

Food is not good or bad. It's just food! However, people who have problems with food tend to feel that their goodness or badness as human beings is directly related to what food they eat and what size their bodies are. They think that people who eat fattening foods and have large bodies are bad, lazy, and disgusting. In contrast, they think that people who eat low-fat foods and have thin bodies are good, valuable, and attractive. Because most compulsive eaters enjoy high-fat foods and have large bodies, this way of thinking usually leads to problems of low self-esteem, self-abuse, guilt, and shame.

Food and Control

Babies eat when they are hungry. They cry, and their parents feed them. They will eat as much food as they need, and then stop. As children get older, many different factors demand that they eat at certain times. Kids in school are not allowed to eat until the lunch bell rings, and kids at home are not allowed to eat

As you grow older, you will begin to take responsibility for your own food choices.

until mealtime. In addition, many children are told that they must finish all of the food on their plates, whether they are hungry for it or not. When they finish, they are told that they are good.

Sometimes, adults reward children for good behavior by giving them candy, baking cookies, or taking them out for ice cream. In contrast, adults often punish children by making them skip a meal or telling them that they can't have any dessert. As a result, young children begin to learn at an early age not to trust their own hunger. Somebody else controls what, when, and how much they eat.

When children become teenagers, their parents usually allow them more control over what they eat. Teens sometimes help to grocery-shop or to prepare dinner. They may have an allowance or a part-time job that allows them to buy snacks or go out to eat with friends. Some buy themselves healthy snacks, but most prefer junk food, particularly if it is forbidden at home.

During this time of greater personal responsibility, teens also find themselves facing at least some of the difficult problems that come with freedom: changing relationships with parents, feelings of loneliness and insecurity, difficulty with managing school work and social or extracurricular activities, anxiety about the future, and confusion about sexuality. Teens have different ways of trying to cope with these problems. Some talk to family or friends, others turn to drugs or alcohol. Teens who suffer from compulsive eating turn to food. It is easier to feel "out of control" about food than it is to feel "out of control" about the problems in your life.

What Is Compulsive Eating?

3

Are you a compulsive eater?
Most people overeat now and
then, and that's normal. But if
you often eat until you are
overstuffed, or you eat large
amounts of food when you
are not really hungry or it's
not a regular mealtime, you
may be a compulsive
eater. A compul-
sive-eating dis-
order left
untreated
can lead to
serious
health
prolems,
such as
a risk
of

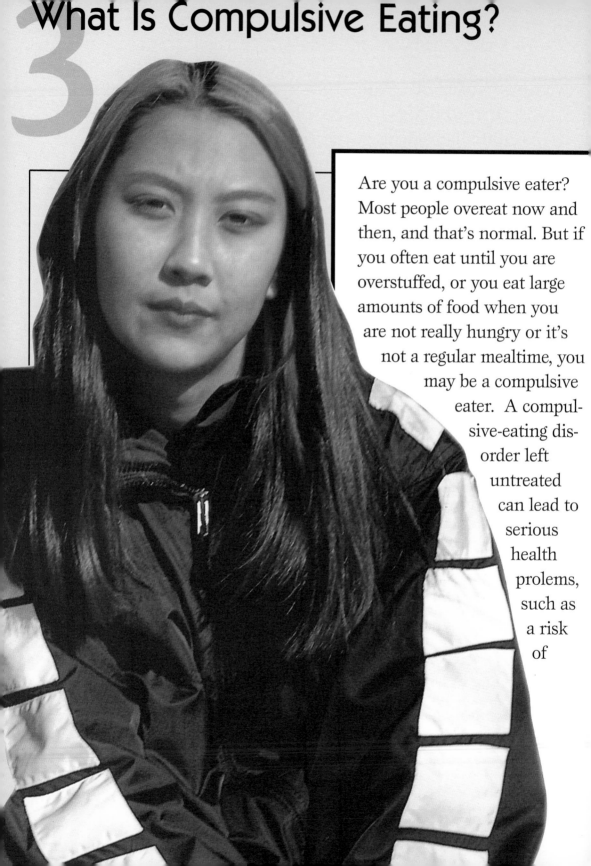

high blood pressure, heart disease, and diabetes, as well as psychological problems. It is important to determine as early as possible whether there is a problem. The earlier it is identified, the sooner the problem can be treated.

Do I Have a Problem?

You may be a compulsive eater if you:

- ❑ Never stop thinking about food.
- ❑ Have trouble recognizing when your body is really hungry and usually eat well beyond the point of fullness.
- ❑ Eat large amounts of food, often in a short period of time, and always finish everything, whether you're hungry or not.
- ❑ Use food to avoid doing things you don't want to do, to manage stressful situations, and to comfort yourself when you're feeling sad, angry, lonely, bored, nervous, or scared.
- ❑ Prefer to eat alone, or you hide food and eat it secretly.
- ❑ Go on and off diets, repeatedly losing and gaining back large amounts of weight.
- ❑ Feel "out of control" when you eat.

□ Judge yourself as "good" or "bad" according to what foods you eat and what size you are.
□ Feel ashamed of or disgusted by your body and your eating habits.
□ Think of eating as one of your only pleasures in life, yet feel guilty about it.

Eating When Your Stomach Isn't Hungry

Experts note that there are two types of hunger: physical and emotional. Physical hunger is the slight discomfort or burning feeling you get in your stomach when it is empty and in need of food. This is a normal and healthy signal that lets you know when it's time to eat. Emotional hunger, on the other hand, has little to do with the body's physical needs. When people experience emotional hunger, they eat to try to fill an emptiness they feel in their hearts and minds.

Because compulsive eaters have learned to eat in response to their emotional needs instead of their physical needs, they often reach a point at which they are no longer able to experience and recognize real hunger. With the messages between the brain and the stomach short-circuited, compulsive eaters continue to think that they are hungry even after

Turning to food in response to emotional stress may be one sign of compulsive eating.

eating too much. Overeating often leads to weight gain, and weight gain usually leads to more of the same painful feelings that caused the person to turn to food in the first place.

Types of Compulsive Eating

The three common patterns of compulsive eating are: secretive snacking, grazing, and binge eating. Some compulsive eaters may have all of these eating habits; others may have just one or two.

Secretive Snacking

When Kathy was thirteen, she started at a new junior high school. None of her old school friends were there to support her. She often found herself sitting alone at a corner table during lunch period. This made her so uncomfortable that she sometimes skipped lunch and hid in the girls' room until the bell rang.

Kathy had been a bit overweight as a child. As a teenager she noticed that she had grown larger than most of the other girls in her class. She felt ashamed of her body. She started to wear big sweaters, and to make excuses so she wouldn't have to change for gym class.

Kathy's mother, who had been thin and popular as a child, thought that if Kathy lost weight she might be able to make friends and gain some confidence. She found a diet in a magazine that she showed to Kathy.

At first Kathy was very excited about dieting. After a few weeks she started to lose some weight. However, her situation at school did not change. She still felt lonely, and she didn't want to sit with anyone in the cafeteria while she ate diet food. Worst of all, Kathy was hungry all the time, but she was reluctant to ask her mother for more food because she didn't want to disappoint her.

Late one night, Kathy got out of bed to use the bathroom.

Her stomach was growling. She tiptoed downstairs and ate a leftover chicken leg she found in the refrigerator. She felt better immediately. She went back to bed and slept through the night. After that, Kathy started sneaking food whenever her mother wasn't looking. She'd get up and fix herself peanut butter sandwiches after everyone had gone to bed, or she'd sneak into the kitchen in the middle of the day and eat just a little bit of all the leftovers in the refrigerator so that nobody would notice the missing food.

Soon Kathy's mother started to ask her why she was gaining back weight. She talked about Kathy's weight all the time, and reduced Kathy's meals with the family to smaller and smaller portions. The more Kathy's mother criticized her daughter's

Compulsive eaters often eat in secret because they feel ashamed about their actions.

weight problem, the more Kathy enjoyed sneaking snacks behind her mother's back.

Kathy is a compulsive eater who uses secretive snacking—eating snacks secretly, often late at night—as her main pattern of food abuse. Kathy feels hungry all the time because of her strict diet, but she also feels too guilty and ashamed to let others see her eating more food. She eats secretly because she doesn't want her mother to know that she is breaking her diet, but eating secretly also makes her feel powerful. Kathy is angry at her mother for making her follow a strict diet, but she is also afraid that her mother's love depends on whether she is fat or thin. Kathy can't express her anger directly, so she gets back at her mother by disobeying her.

Grazing

Craig, fourteen, was always bigger than the rest of the students in his class. As a little kid, he had been the last boy to be chosen for teams in gym class. And the team that got him would complain about his lack of coordination and skill. When Craig got to high school, though, the football coach noticed his large build and suggested that he join the school team.

At first Craig told the coach that he wasn't very good at sports, but the coach said that the team needed offensive linemen who, like Craig, were big, solid, and pow-

erful. The coach also explained that weight training would help Craig build up his strength.

Craig was convinced. He thought football might be a good way for him to make more friends and to show he could be good at sports. He spent the summer before his sophomore year eating more than ever, drinking power shakes, studying videos about football, and lifting weights at the local YMCA. His weight ballooned up to nearly 230 pounds.

When Craig showed up for football training in August, all the guys on the team were amazed to see how much he had bulked up. He was bigger than ever but looked powerful. He joined the team and played successfully. Craig was so big and strong, and such a big eater, that he soon earned the nickname "Ox." At lunch, kids would sit at his table and make bets on how much he could eat.

Craig soon found himself eating constantly—snacking on candy bars between classes, munching cookies in the locker room before and after practice, eating at home in front of the open refrigerator door while talking to friends on the phone. Craig's mother worried about her son's weight gain, but Craig's father told her that she shouldn't be concerned because their son was a football star.

By the end of his sophomore year, Craig weighed nearly 270 pounds. Because of his elevated blood pressure and high cholesterol count, the coach told him he wouldn't be able to play football again in the fall.

Craig is a compulsive eater who uses grazing—overeating at different times and places throughout the day—as his main pattern of food abuse. Unlike Kathy, Craig does not appear to be ashamed of overeating because he does it in front of people. But inside, he does not feel good about what he does. He suffers from low self-esteem, and he uses food to gain attention and acceptance, instead of letting people get to know the real person inside the body.

Binge Eating

Anna, fifteen, was a bright girl with many friends. She had a great sense of humor and was always joking around, making people laugh. Anna was overweight, but none of her friends ever mentioned it to her because it never seemed important.

However, Anna had a secret: her home life was not happy. Anna was an only child. Her mother had died when she was ten, and she lived alone with her father. Anna's father sometimes drank too much, and when he was drunk he often became violent. He said cruel things to Anna, and even threatened to hit her.

Whenever this happened, Anna would run upstairs, lock herself in her room, and turn up the television really loud. Then she'd take out the supply of candy, cookies, cakes, and potato chips she kept hidden under her bed and on the top shelf in her closet. While her father yelled and threw things downstairs, Anna would open two or three large bags of potato chips and eat all of them without stopping. Sometimes she would devour three or four packages of chocolate chip cookies or several boxes of cupcakes. As Anna ate, she would stop feeling afraid about what her father was doing downstairs. All she would think about was eating.

Anna would eat like this for one or two hours, depending on how much her father had upset her. When she finished, she usually felt tired and disappointed. She would hide all of the empty bags, boxes, and wrappers under her bed, turn off the light, and try to sleep. However, Anna usually had trouble falling asleep. She would begin to talk to herself in her head. She'd tell herself that she was fat, ugly, disgusting, and out of control, and she would often end up crying herself to sleep.

The next day, Anna would go down to breakfast, and she and her father would both pretend that nothing bad had happened the previous night. Anna would go to school, tell jokes and make her friends laugh, and everyone would think all was normal.

Anna is a compulsive eater who uses binge eating—eating unusually large amounts of food in a short period of time—as her main pattern of food abuse. Anna binges as a reaction to her father's alcoholism. Because she can't talk about her problems with her friends or deal with her father's drinking,

Anna uses bingeing as a way to escape the fear and anger she feels when her father loses control.

The relief that she feels while bingeing is only temporary. Anna always ends up criticizing and blaming herself. And, unfortunately, when she stops eating, her situation at home is still the same.

The Dangers of Dieting

Many compulsive eaters believe that dieting is the answer to all of their problems. They tell themselves that if they find the right diet and lose weight, all of their problems will disappear and their lives will be perfect.

It's important to find other ways to relieve uncomfortable feelings. Exercise is a great way to get rid of stress.

Diets are not a magical cure for the problems faced by compulsive eaters or anyone else. In fact, dieting can be very dangerous. Compulsive eaters do not understand their own bodily needs, and diets make the problem worse because dieters must eat according to a strict plan that somebody else has designed for them. These plans usually list "good" and "bad" foods, and they often instruct the dieter to eat much less than the body needs to function properly.

Actually, drastically cutting calories can sabotage weight loss. When the body suddenly receives fewer calories than it needs, it tries to protect itself from starvation by slowing down the speed at which it burns calories. It also stores extra calories as fat. Furthermore, because dieters force themselves to give up the "bad" foods that they enjoy in favor of small quantities of "good" foods, it is inevitable that the diet will be broken. Most people who deny their bodies certain foods will ultimately go off of a diet. When they do "cheat," they often binge eat. While going off of a diet is a normal, even healthy reaction to the restrictions of most diets, compulsive eaters usually can't forgive themselves for doing it. They see their action as yet another failure.

The worst thing about dieting is that it can be dangerous to your health. Not every diet will develop into an eating disorder, but studies have found that 80 percent of all eating disorders started with a diet.

Causes of Compulsive Eating

4

Compulsive eaters abuse
food for many reasons
and all of them have to
do with negative self-
image. Compulsive
eaters
feel

they are not good enough, that nobody could love them as they are, and that they have no self-control. They feel that their fat makes them unworthy of a good life, and they abuse food to avoid dealing directly with their problems.

Eating Instead of Feeling

Compulsive eaters try to swallow their emotions by swallowing food. Most of us don't want to experience anger, loneliness, confusion, or fear, but compulsive eaters attempt to avoid these feelings by focusing all of their emotions around food and weight issues. The unhappiness that comes from overeating, they believe, is easier to deal with than other bad feelings. This is unhealthy because the real pain does not disappear; it hides deep inside and becomes more and more difficult to face.

Loneliness

"Everybody at school seems to have a boyfriend or girlfriend, but nobody will ever love me because I'm fat and ugly."

"You can't trust people anyway. They are never there for you when you need them. Food is the one thing I can count on in my life."

Many compulsive eaters have not experienced enough love in their lives, so they begin to think of

Compulsive eaters may isolate themselves from friends and avoid social activities.

food as love. They may grow up in families where everybody is expected to be an overachiever, and they feel pressured to be "perfect." Or their parents and/or brothers and sisters may be overly critical, always pointing out what is wrong with them and never what is right. In still other instances, family members are not allowed to recognize or express their emotions, particularly feelings of warmth and affection. When people do not have a chance to learn how to have healthy, loving relationships with others, they often turn to a compulsion, in this case food, to fill the emptiness and loneliness in their lives.

Confusion

"I don't like boys to pay too much attention to me. It makes me feel uncomfortable! When I was thin, boys used to look at me and make embarrassing comments. Now that I've gained weight they leave me alone, but I've stopped doing a lot of the things I used to do, like playing sports and going to school dances. I won't swim at the town pool because everybody would laugh at me in my bathing suit. I'd rather hang out at home and watch TV anyway. Who needs all that stuff?"

Growing up isn't easy. Teens must learn to be responsible for themselves and their actions. Sexuality is one of the toughest issues most teens face. Being sexually attracted to other people is both exciting and scary. Some compulsive eaters use food abuse and weight gain to protect themselves from feelings that are new and difficult to understand. Weight gain is often an excuse for compulsive eaters to avoid developing relationships that might lead to sexual feelings and situations.

Fear

"I wanted to join the drama club, but I'm afraid everyone will make fun of me and tell me I'm not attractive

enough to be on stage. I almost went to audition after school, but then I chickened out. Instead, I went home and ate a whole pizza."

Compulsive eaters may also use their weight to avoid other challenges when they're afraid of failure. Instead of joining in on activities that will help them meet new people, or trying new things that will help them learn about life, they convince themselves that they never had any chance of being successful or accepted because they are fat. They turn to food to calm their fears. Food can't judge them or tell them they aren't good enough.

When compulsive eaters avoid new challenges, they can miss out on exciting experiences.

Anger

"Sometimes I get so mad I don't know what to do with myself. I sit in my room and eat and eat until I can't feel anything anymore."

It's not easy to express anger. There are many people who don't like to have confrontations and will do anything to avoid them. Some people feel that they don't have a right to get angry or think they'll lose people in their lives if they get angry at them. But anger is a healthy emotion. If it's not expressed, it just builds inside a person. Some people deal with their anger through compulsive eating. But food doesn't and can't make the anger go away. The anger is still there; it's just buried deeper inside.

Compulsive eaters are inclined to think that they'll never find solutions to their problems with food abuse and weight gain. However, this is not so. If they learn to make some important changes in attitude and behavior, they can indeed live healthier, happier lives. Many people who have struggled with compulsive eating have recovered and achieved healthy relationships with food. You can too.

5 Changing Your Relationship with Food and Yourself

If you are a compulsive eater, chances are that you are much kinder and more supportive to other people than you are to yourself.

Compulsive eaters suffer from low self-esteem; they don't always believe in their own value as human beings. Be aware of when you are being unkind to yourself and work on changing. Here are four ways to avoid negative thinking:

❑ DON'T criticize yourself! It's difficult to make your life better tomorrow if you hate who you are today. The next time you find yourself saying or thinking something unkind about yourself or your body, stop and think whether you would ever say such a mean thing to a family member or a friend. Chances are you wouldn't. You probably don't like to hurt other people's feelings, so why hurt your own? Try to be more aware of frustrating, self-critical thoughts, and take a moment to apologize to yourself when you hurt yourself. Also try to admire yourself for the good qualities you have that don't revolve around appearance, such as intelligence, generosity, thoughtfulness, kindness, and a sense of humor.

❑ DON'T compare yourself to others! To the compulsive eater, other people always seem thinner, happier, more successful. Thin people seem to live easy lives, free of the pain and shame that the compulsive eater must cope with every day. However, remember that appearances can be deceiving. All people experience struggles and suffer disappointments, but you can't always see this in the people you admire or envy.

❑ DON'T worry about what other people think! Compulsive eaters spend too much time and energy thinking about other people's opinions, real or imagined. They assume the worst, believing that others will probably reject them or make fun of them because they're fat. This negative view often prevents compulsive eaters from meeting new friends and participating in fun and interesting activities that they want to try.

Some people may treat you badly because of your weight, but others won't. Focus on the people you meet who don't focus on your weight. There will always be unhappy people in the world who feel the need to reject or abuse anyone who is different, but most people are more open-minded and caring. Besides, it's impossible to know what everyone else thinks and feels about us. Even if we did know, we couldn't necessarily control or change it. All that time worrying about who likes you and who doesn't like you is better spent learning to love and care for yourself, and finding friends who like you for who you are.

❐ DON'T live in the future! Nearly every compulsive eater thinks, "If only I were thin!" They dream of some magical day in the future when they'll wake up and find themselves thin and happy. They believe that all of their problems would disappear if they could just lose weight and keep it off. Sadly, this is a false hope. If you are a compulsive eater, you must learn to live in the present instead of living for the future, and that means finding a way to love, respect, and accept the most important person in your life: the person you are today! That also means understanding that thinness does not equal happiness.

Making Peace with Food

One of the keys to overcoming compulsive eating is to learn how to pay closer attention to where, when, what, and how much you are eating. The ideas on the following pages were adapted from exercises developed by Dr. Jon Kabat-Zinn and Dr. Elizabeth Wheeler at the University of Massachusetts Medical Center's Stress Reduction Clinic.

Keeping a food diary is an excellent way to discover how food and eating make you feel.

Where Do You Eat?

Do you usually eat while hiding alone in your room? Sitting in front of the TV? Standing by the refrigerator? If so, such habits may be part of your problem. If you eat alone, you are probably full of negative feelings, making you more likely to overeat. If you choose to eat while doing something else, you are probably eating "on automatic," which means that you eat everything without paying attention to either the food or the needs of your body.

Instead, try eating at a kitchen or dining room table. Whenever possible, eat with other people.

Eating is a normal and pleasurable activity, and you shouldn't feel ashamed or embarrassed about it.

When Do You Eat?

Do you eat all day long? After school? Late at night? Do you eat when you feel lonely? Angry? Sad? Nervous? Bored? Because compulsive eaters usually overeat as a reaction to powerful feelings, it is important to try to recognize when this is happening and find healthier ways to deal with stressful situations.

One way to learn about your own eating patterns is to keep a food diary. This could be a notebook in which you write the date and time, list the names and amounts of foods you eat, and state thoughts or feelings before, during, and after eating. After a while, you will be able to look at your diary and see if there are certain situations or feelings that often cause you to overeat.

Maybe you overeat when you're anxious about an upcoming test. Instead of smothering your anxiety with food, which won't make matters better anyhow, take a breather. Do some relaxation exercises. Call a friend and talk. Take a bath. Turn on some calming music.

Have an argument with a friend? Walk around the block to calm yourself down. Turn up the stereo and dance. Clean your room. Put your gripes down on

It may be hard to break certain habits because they provide compulsive eaters with a temporary sense of comfort.

paper, then tear up the paper and throw it away along with your anger.

Bored? Lonely? Pick up the phone. Invite someone over. Write a letter to a close relative. Join a class and learn something new.

What and How Much Do You Eat?

Do you crave certain comfort foods when you're having a difficult day? Do you always eat until you feel sick? With a little more awareness, it is possible to tune in to what your body really needs and to make healthy choices when selecting foods to eat.

Start by paying attention to when your body is and isn't hungry. Try not to eat at all until you get the empty feeling that is your stomach's signal for food, then don't hesitate to satisfy that hunger.

Another way to get back in touch with your body's real needs is to try eating slowly and thoughtfully at regular mealtimes. Before you eat, take a few moments to breathe deeply and concentrate on how you feel. Look at the food that you're going to eat, and think about where it came from, how it was prepared, and how it will nourish you. Once you've been eating, stop halfway through the meal and take a break, paying attention to how you feel. Have you had enough? If not, keep eating slowly and carefully. If so, say to yourself, "I've had enough food and I'm finished," and push your plate away.

If you keep eating and finish everything on your plate, take a moment (about ten minutes after you've finished eating) and think about how you feel one last time. Do you feel good or bad? Satisfied or too full? If you feel bad or too full, don't be angry at yourself. Just remember that it takes time to relearn your internal hunger signals, but that you do have the power to stop eating when you feel satisfied.

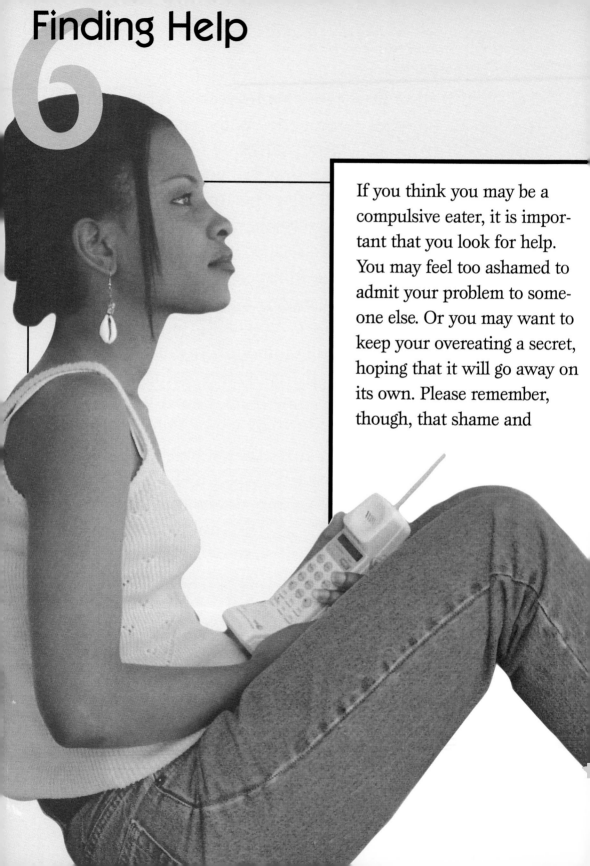

Finding Help

6

If you think you may be a compulsive eater, it is important that you look for help. You may feel too ashamed to admit your problem to someone else. Or you may want to keep your overeating a secret, hoping that it will go away on its own. Please remember, though, that shame and secrecy are two indicators of compulsive eating and that no problem ever disappears if you don't face it honestly. Asking for help is not a sign of weakness. It is a way of showing that you love yourself and are ready to trust others to help you become the best person you can be.

Treatment Options

There are many different programs and techniques designed to treat compulsive eating. Each one has a different approach. It's important to try and find the program that's right for you. Some people overcome overeating by reading self-help books. There are many books available in your local library or book-store. You'll find helpful resources at the end of this book as well. Other people, though, may feel that their compulsive eating is really out of control. In that case, a person should consider seeing a thera-pist and a registered dietitian for help.

Most dietitians will help you relearn your internal hunger signals. They will work with you in individual counseling sessions. This process takes time, but many people have been treated successfully. The therapist will help you uncover some of the reasons behind your compulsive eating. Eating disorders are complex prob-lems. They are caused by a combination of many fac-tors, including psychological issues, biological changes, family influences, and messages from society.

The first thing to do is talk to someone you trust. This person might be a friend, a parent, a sibling, or a teacher. If there is something going on in your life that is bothering you or causing you pain, tell that person about it. He or she will listen without judging you and will help you as much as possible.

You may find it easier to accept help from someone you don't know personally. Your school guidance office is a good place to start. Guidance counselors are caring people who understand the difficulties faced by teens. Food-related problems have become common among teenagers, and many guidance counselors are now quite knowledgeable about compulsive eating. If not, your guidance counselor will be able to direct you to a specialist who is. The counselor might also suggest a support group where you can meet other teens who share your problems and concerns. Support groups are important because they help people understand that they are not alone in facing their problems.

Recovering from an eating disorder is like fighting an addiction to drugs or alcohol. It is a long, slow, and difficult process, and it may never be 100 percent complete. A recovering alcoholic will always have to be careful. Even if she hasn't had a drink in years, she may always have a strong urge to drink. People with eating disorders also have ongoing struggles and may relapse many times. But with treatment,

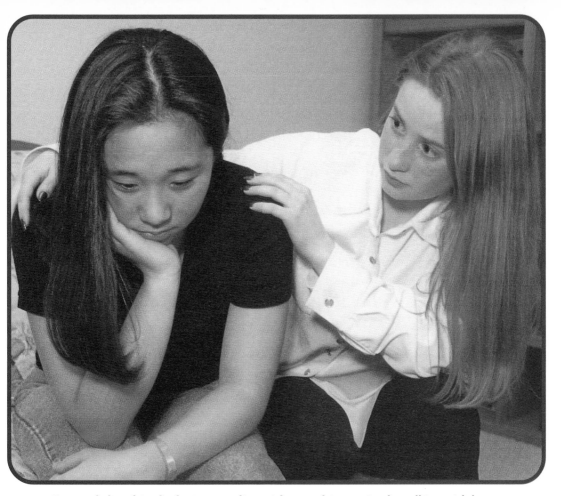
You can help a friend who is struggling with compulsive eating by talking with her and offering your support.

many people do recover and go on to lead happy, fulfilling lives. If you are suffering from compulsive eating, please consider getting help.

Helping a Friend

If you think a friend or family member is a compulsive eater, talk to him or her about it. Speak in a way that is loving and supportive, and let the person know that you are there to help. Share some of the information you have learned about compulsive eating. If you want to know more, try contacting some of the organizations listed in the Where to Go for Help section at the end of this book.

Because facing such a difficult problem can be extremely painful, your friend or loved one may not be willing to accept your help when it is first offered. Don't be hurt if the person becomes angry or resentful, and don't try to force him or her to accept your help immediately. Unfortunately, you cannot force a person to get help if he or she does not want it or is not ready for it. If that happens, offer to continue to listen and care, and perhaps one day that person will be ready to talk openly about his or her feelings and take that first step toward recovery.

Your Future

Reading this book is the first step toward understanding the reasons behind compulsive eating. Working to develop a healthy relationship with food and a positive self-image are two very important aspects of your life.

These are not easy things to do, however. Even after we recognize the different influences on our eating habits and self-image, it is still difficult to accept ourselves as we are. This is because we still have to function in a world that sends us mixed messages about food and dangerous messages about body shape and size. But that doesn't mean we shouldn't continue to try to eat in a healthy way and feel good about ourselves.

In fact, you can make changes now that will benefit you in the future. The choices and decisions that you make today can give you a foundation for facing the many challenges in the years to come. Accepting yourself and learning to appreciate all the individual qualities that make you a unique person will give you the strength and confidence you need to excel in all aspects of your life.

Glossary

addiction A compulsive or obsessive need for and use of a substance.

anorexia nervosa An eating disorder in which a person has an intense fear of getting fat, refuses to eat, and keeps losing weight.

bingeing Rapid eating of large amounts of food—2000 calories or more—during a short period of time.

biological Based in your body, your physical being.

bulimia nervosa An eating disorder in which huge amounts of food are eaten, then purged by vomiting, using laxatives, or exercising excessively.

compulsive A compulsion is an urge that you have great difficulty resisting. Compulsive eating is an irresistible urge to eat.

culture Beliefs, accomplishments, and behavior patterns of a community or population, passed on from one generation to another.

grazing Overeating at different times and places throughout the day.

ideal A standard of perfection. In relation to the body, it is often impossible and unhealthy to achieve.

influences Outside forces, including family, peers, and society, that encourage you to believe or do things.

myth An idea or story that many people believe but that is not true.

obsession Something you cannot stop thinking or worrying about.

psychological Based in your mind; your thinking and understanding of the events and people in your life.

self-esteem The way you see and treat yourself based on your own confidence in and respect for yourself. Also, the feeling that you are someone who deserves to be liked and respected by others.

sensual Appealing to any or all of the five senses: sight, touch, taste, smell, and hearing.

yo-yo dieting A habit of losing weight by dieting, followed by regaining weight, and often repeating this pattern.

Where to Go for Help

American Dietetic Association
216 West Jackson Boulevard, Suite 805
Chicago, IL 60606
(312) 899-0040
Nutrition hotline: (800) 366-1655
Web site: http://www.eatright.org

Anorexia Nervosa and Related Eating Disorders, Inc. (ANRED)
P.O. Box 5102
Eugene, OR 97405
(541) 344-1144
Web site: http://www.anred.com

Eating Disorders Awareness and Prevention, Inc. (EDAP)
603 Stewart Street, Suite 803
Seattle, WA 98101
(206) 382-3587
Web site: http://members.aol.com/edapinc

Gürze Books
P.O. Box 2238
Carlsbad, CA 92018-9883
(800) 756-7533
Web site: http://www.gurze.com

National Assocation of Anorexia Nervosa and Associated Disorders (ANAD)
Box 7
Highland Park, IL 60035
(847) 831-3438
Web site: http://members.aol.com/anad20/index.html

National Eating Disorders Organization (NEDO)
6655 South Yale Avenue
Tulsa, OK 74136
(918) 481-4044
Web site: http://www.laureate.com

Overeaters Anonymous Headquarters
P.O. Box 44020
Rio Rancho, NM 87174-4020
(505) 891-2664
Web site: http://www.overeatersanonymous.org

In Canada

Anorexia Nervosa and Associated Disorders (ANAD)
109 - 2040 West 12th Avenue
Vancouver, BC V6J 2G2
(604) 739-2070

The National Eating Disorder Information Centre
College Wing 1st Floor, Room 211
200 Elizabeth Street
Toronto, ON M5G 2C4
(416) 340-4156

Web sites

The Body Shop. A Web site dedicated to improving the self-esteem and self-respect of all people.
http://www.the-body-shop.com

Go, girl! Magazine. An online fitness magazine full of positive information and images for young women. http://www.gogirlmag.com

gURL. An online zine for young women with good straight talk about body image.
http://www.gurl.com

For Further Reading

Berry, Joy. *Good Answers to Tough Questions About Weight Problems and Eating Disorders.* Chicago: Children's Press, 1990.

Cooke, Kaz. *Real Gorgeous: The Truth About Body and Beauty.* New York: W. W. Norton, 1996.

Crook, Marion. *Looking Good: Teenagers and Eating Disorders.* Toronto: NC Press, Ltd., 1992.

Folkers, Gladys, and Jeanne Engelman. *Taking Charge of My Mind and Body: A Girls' Guide to Outsmarting Alcohol, Drugs, Smoking, and Eating Problems.* Minneapolis: Free Spirit Publishing, 1997.

Kano, Susan. *Making Peace with Food.* New York: HarperCollins, 1989.

Kolodny, Nancy J. *When Food's a Foe: How You Can Confront and Conquer Your Eating Disorder.* New York: Little, Brown and Company, 1992.

Roth, Geneen. *Breaking Free from Compulsive Eating.* New York: Plume Books, 1993.

Siegel, Michele, Judith Brisman, and Margot
Weinshel. *Surviving an Eating Disorder: New
Perspectives and Strategies for Family and
Friends.* New York: HarperCollins, 1997.

The following books can be ordered directly from
Gürze Books. They will be sent in a plain, confi-
dential package.

Cohen, Mary Anne. *French Toast for Breakfast:
Declaring Peace with Emotional Eating.*
Hall, Lindsey (ed.) *Full Lives: Women Who Have
Freed Themselves from Food and Weight
Obsession.*
———. *Bulimia: A Guide to Recovery.*
Zerbe, Kathryn. *The Body Betrayed: A Deeper
Understanding of Women, Eating Disorders, and
Treatment.*

Index

About the Author

Christie Ward has a Master of Arts degree in English/Creative Writing and has worked as a part-time composition and literature instructor at community colleges. After working as a volunteer English instructor in Central Europe, she returned to the United States and earned a Master of Arts degree in Teaching English to Speakers of Other Languages. She currently lives and teaches in Connecticut.

Design and Layout: Christine Innamorato

Consulting Editor: Michele I. Drohan

Photo Credits

p.10 by John Bentham; p.16 © Ron Chapple/FPG International; p. 20 © Joe Viesti/Viesti Associates, Inc.; pp.24, 46 by Ira Fox; p. 36 © Skjold Photographs; p.40 © Kevin Vandiviez/Viesti Associates, Inc.; p. 42 © Dennie Cody/FPG International; p. 50 © James Davis/International Stock; All other photos by Bonnie Rothstein-Brewer.